Jesus
His Resurrection

Matthew 27:54-66, 28:1-20
Mark 15:42-47, 16:1-20
Luke 23:50-56, 24:1-49 and 50-53
John 19:38-42, 20:1-31, 21:1-25

by
Rebecca Daniel

illustrated by
Nancee McClure

A Christian Education Activity Book

Cover by Dan Grossmann

ISBN No. 0-86653-233-1
Printing No. 98765

Shining Star Publications
A Division of Good Apple, Inc.
Box 299
Carthage, IL 62321-0299

NOTE: The activities in this book were written using the King James Version of the Bible, so always use this version to solve the puzzles.

INTRODUCTION

After Jesus died on the cross, some of His persecutors realized His divinity. "Now when the centurion, and they that were with him, watching Jesus, saw the earthquake, and those things that were done, they feared greatly, saying, Truly this was the Son of God."

A rich man named Joseph went to Pilate and begged for the body of Jesus. Pilate commanded the body be delivered. "And when Joseph had taken the body, he wrapped it in a clean linen cloth, And laid it in his own new tomb, which he had hewn out in the rock: and he rolled a great stone to the door of the sepulchre, and departed."

The next day the chief priests and Pharisees went to Pilate saying, "We remember that that deceiver said, while he was yet alive, After three days I will rise again. Command therefore that the sepulchre be made sure until the third day, lest his disciples come by night, and steal him away. . . ." Pilate agreed and "So they went, and made the sepulchre sure, sealing the stone, and setting a watch."

On the morning of the third day an angel descended and rolled the heavy stone aside. The guards were terrified and rushed back to the city. Mary Magdalene and some other women hurried to the tomb with spices to anoint Jesus' body. When Mary saw the open tomb, she rushed off to tell Peter and John. The other women entered the open tomb. An angel told them, "He is not here: for he is risen, as he said. Come, see the place where the Lord lay. And go quickly, and tell his disciples that he is risen from the dead . . . he goeth before you into Galilee; there shall ye see him. . . ."

As they hurried to tell the disciples the good news, they met Jesus on the road. Jesus said, "All hail . . . Be not afraid: go tell my brethren that they go into Galilee, and there shall they see me."

The guards had reached the city by this time and told what they had witnessed. The elders didn't want people to know that Jesus had fulfilled His prophecy to rise on the third day. So a large amount of money was given to the soldiers as a bribe. The soldiers were told to say that the disciples had taken Jesus' body from the tomb. "So they took the money, and did as they were taught. . . ."

All the disciples except Thomas went into Galilee to a mountain to wait for Jesus. "And when they saw him, they worshipped him: but some doubted." Jesus told the disciples, "Go ye therefore, and teach all nations, baptizing them in the name of the Father, and of the Son, and of the Holy Ghost: Teaching them to observe all things whatsoever I have commanded you: and, lo, I am with you alway, even unto the end of the world."

When the eleven disciples saw Thomas, they told him they had seen and spoken to Jesus. Thomas didn't believe them. He said, "Except I shall see in his hands the print of the nails . . . I will not believe." Eight days later, Thomas and the other disciples saw Jesus again. Jesus told Thomas, "Reach hither thy finger, and behold my hands. . . ." Thomas answered and said unto Him, "My Lord and my God." Then Jesus spoke to Thomas about faith. "Thomas, because thou hast seen me, thou hast believed: blessed are they that have not seen, and yet have believed."

While fishing in the sea of Tiberias, the disciples were disappointed because they had not caught even one fish. Jesus stood on the shore, but the disciples did not know it was the Lord. "Then Jesus saith unto them, Children, have ye any meat? They answered him, No." Then Jesus told them to cast their nets on the right side of the ship. "They cast therefore, and now they were not able to draw it for the multitude of fishes." Then the disciples knew that it was Jesus speaking to them.

John 21:25 says that there are so many things which Jesus did "the which, if they should be written every one, I suppose that even the world itself could not contain the books that should be written."

BURIAL OF JESUS

Matthew 27:54-59; Mark 15:42-47; Luke 23:50-56; John 19:38-42

Find the shortest path through the maze. Color the path. To discover the message, write the letters in the order they are found.

SECRET MESSAGE: _ _ _ _ _ _ _ _

_ _   _ _ _ _ _ _ _ _ _ _ _ _ _ _ _

Name______________________________

Begin in the upper left-hand corner and end in the lower right-hand corner. Find a path through the letters that spells a message. You must move across or down. You may not move diagonally.

SECRET MESSAGE: _____

_______ ____________

_______.

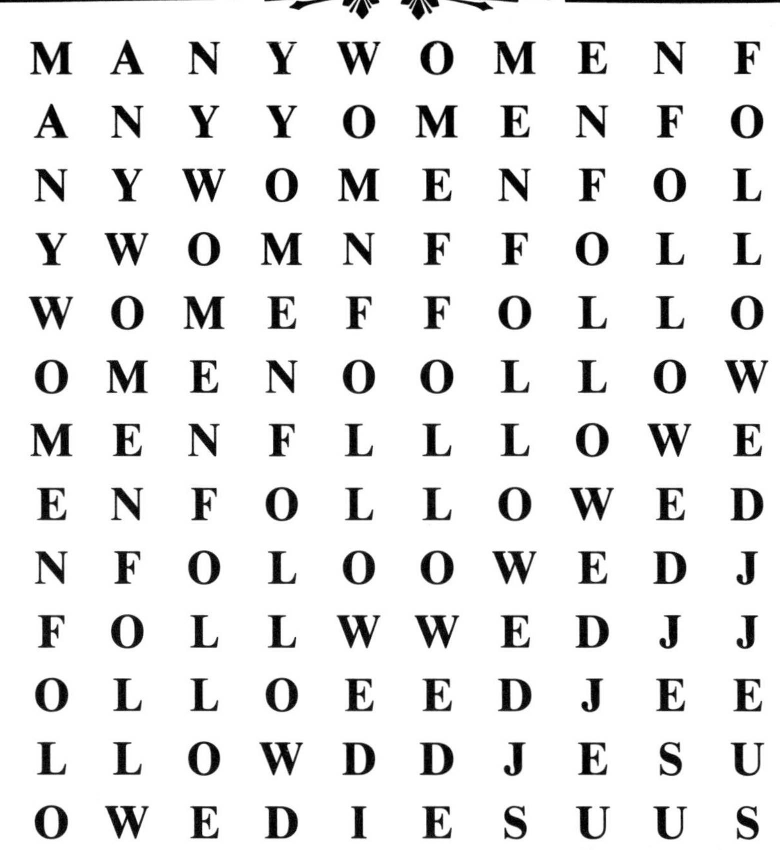

M	A	N	Y	W	O	M	E	N	F
A	N	Y	Y	O	M	E	N	F	O
N	Y	W	O	M	E	N	F	O	L
Y	W	O	M	N	F	F	O	L	L
W	O	M	E	F	F	O	L	L	O
O	M	E	N	O	O	L	L	O	W
M	E	N	F	L	L	L	O	W	E
E	N	F	O	L	L	O	W	E	D
N	F	O	L	O	O	W	E	D	J
F	O	L	L	W	W	E	D	J	J
O	L	L	O	E	E	D	J	E	E
L	L	O	W	D	D	J	E	S	U
O	W	E	D	I	E	S	U	U	S

What word found in the Scriptures can you put in the top row that makes three-letter words of the letters going down?

a	l	o	c	e	e	a	o	t	o	o
n	l	t	e	e	a	t	w	s	w	t

Name_______________________________________

SEALING THE SEPULCHRE

Matthew 27:60-66

Complete each word by adding one letter. The words are all found in the Scriptures. Then read down to discover the secret message.

SECRET MESSAGE: "_ _ _ _ _ _

_ _ _ _ _ _ _ _ _ _ _ _ _ _ _ _ _ _ _ _

_ _ _ _ _ _ _ _ _ _ _ _ _."

__nd
there__ore
__omb
b__
su__e

__hat
__im
wo__se
d__ad
y__

ma__e
se__ling
da__
__tone

sett__ng

__ay
r__sen
Pi__ate
sepu__chre

e__ror
f__rst
__hall
th__

M__ry
Ma__dalene
w__s
sitt__ng
agai__st

Name______________________

Let the Scriptures help you solve this puzzle. Fill in the blanks with the correct words. Then place these words in the puzzle.

"Pilate ______ unto ______, Ye have a watch: go your way, ______ it as ______ as ye _____. So they ______, and made the _______________ sure, ___________ the ________, and setting a ________." ***Matthew 27:65,66***

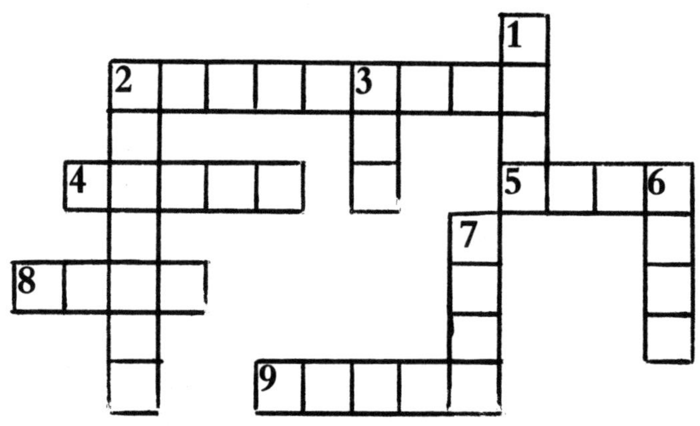

Begin in the lower right-hand box. Draw a continuous line from letter to letter going left, right, up or down. You may not move diagonally. When you finish, the letters should form a sentence.

ANSWER: "_ _ _ _ _   _ _   _ _
_ _ _ _ _   _ _   _ _   _ _ _."

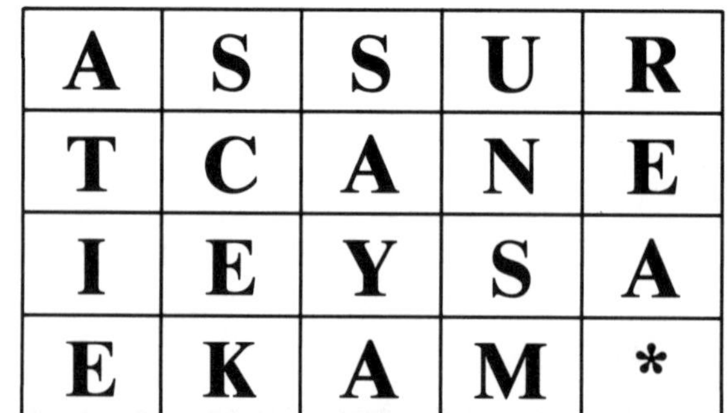

A	S	S	U	R
T	C	A	N	E
I	E	Y	S	A
E	K	A	M	*

Name______________________________________

RESURRECTION OF THE LORD

Matthew 28:1-8; Mark 16:1-14; Luke 24:1-49; John 20:1-23

To discover the secret message, write the letter of the alphabet that comes before each letter found below.

"BOE, CFIPME, UIFSF XBT B

____ ________ ______ _____ _

HSFBU FBSUIRVBLF: GPS UIF

_______ _____________ _____ ____

BOHFM PG UIF MPSE EFTDFOEFE

________ ___ ____ ______ __________

GSPN IFBWFO, BOE DBNF BOE

______ ________ _____ ______ ____

SPMMFE CBDL UIF TUPOF GSPN

_________ ______ ____ _______ ______

UIF EPPS, BOE TBU VQPO

____ _____ _____ _____ ______

JU."

___

Name______________________________

Unscramble the words below and write the secret messsage.

"EH SI TON ERHE: ROF EH SI

___ __ ____ _____ ____ ___ __

SRIEN, SA EH DISA. EMCO, ESE

_____ ___ ___ ____ ______ ____

ETH APLCE EREWH ETH DRLO

____ ______ _______ ____ _____

YLA. DNA OG YCIQUKL, DAN

____ ____ ___ ________ ____

LTEL SIH ECSDIIPLS TATH EH SI

_____ ____ _________ _____ ___ __

SRIEN MOFR EHT DADE. . . ."

_____ _____ ____ _____

Below are three words from the Scriptures. They have been scrambled together. Can you unscramble these three words?

ANSWER: _ _ _ _ _

_ _.

Q I T A R C K H U D L Y D E E P Y E T

Name______________________________

JESUS MEETS HIS DISCIPLES

Matthew 28:9,10

Use the number code to solve this puzzle.

A = 1, B = 2, C = 3, D = 4, E = 5, F = 6, G = 7, H = 8, I = 9, J = 10, K = 11, L = 12, M = 13, N = 14, O = 15, P = 16, Q = 17, R = 18, S = 19, T = 20, U = 21, V = 22, W = 23, X = 24, Y = 25, Z = 26

"1,14,4 1,19 20,8,5,25 23,5,14,20 20,15

20,5,12,12 8,9,19 4,9,19,3,9,16,12,5,19,

2,5,8,15,12,4, 10,5,19,21,19 13,5,20

20,8,5,13, 19,1,25,9,14,7, 1,12,12 8,1,9,12.

1,14,4 20,8,5,25 3,1,13,5 1,14,4 8,5,12,4

8,9,13 2,25 20,8,5 6,5,5,20, 1,14,4

23,15,18,19,8,9,16,16,5,4 8,9,13."

Name____

To discover the secret message, use the consonants listed below and complete the words. Cross out each letter when you have used it.

B D F N R T

“__e __o__ a____ai__.”

B G H L L M N R R T T Y

“__o __e____ ____ ____e______e__.”

G G L L N T

“__o i____o __a__i__ee.”

H H H L L M R S S T T Y

“____e__e ____a____ ____e__ __ee __e.”

The designs below are actually words. Find the hidden letters in each design to form words which will solve this puzzle.

ANSWER: _ _ _ _ _ _ _ _ _ _

_ _ _.

Name______________________________

BRIBING ROMAN GUARDS

Matthew 28:11-17

Place the correct vowel in each blank to spell words and discover the secret message.

TH__ __LD__RS D__DN'T W__NT
P____PL__ T__ KN__W TH__T
J__S__S H__D F__LF__LL__D H__S
PR__PH__CY T__ R__S__ __N TH__
TH__RD D__Y. S__ __ L__RG__
__M____NT __F M__N__Y W__S
G__V__N T__ TH__ S__LD____RS
__S __ BR__B__. TH__ S__LD____RS
W__R__ T__LD T__ T__LL
__V__RY__N__ TH__T TH__
D__SC__PL__S H__D T__K__N
J__S__S' B__DY FR__M TH__
T__MB.

Name______________________________

Decode the secret message. Some of the letters have been replaced with numbers. You must decide which letters stand for which numbers.

B = __ D = __ H = __ M = __ N = __ S = __ T = __ Y = __

"A94 W5E9 35E8 2AW 5I6, 35E8

______ ______ ______ ______ ______ ______

WOR25IPPE4 5I6: 7U3 2O6E

______ ______ ______ ______

4OU73E4."

______

Can you find 10 words in the Scriptures that have homonyms? Write each word and list its homonym.

1.______________ ______________
2.______________ ______________
3.______________ ______________
4.______________ ______________
5.______________ ______________
6.______________ ______________
7.______________ ______________
8.______________ ______________
9.______________ ______________
10.______________ ______________

Name______________________________

TEACH ALL NATIONS

Matthew 28:18-20

To discover the secret message, follow the lines and write the letters in the order they are found.

SECRET MESSAGE: "__ ___

_____ ____ ________."

1 2 3 4 5

y

h

m

I

w

y

u i

a

t

a

l

a

o

w

Name______________________________

Let your Bible help you solve this crossword puzzle.

"Go ye (2 down), and (3 across) all nations, baptizing them in the name of the (1 across), and of the (7 across), and of the (4 down) Ghost: Teaching them to observe all things whatsoever I (8 across) commanded (5 across): and, lo, I am with you (9 down), (10 down) (6 down) the (10 across) of the world. Amen."

Matthew 28:19,20

Name____________________________

JESUS APPEARS TO DISCIPLES

Luke 24:36-49; John 20:19-23

Find and circle every word from the Scriptures hidden in the letter maze below. The words may be written down, across or diagonally.

"And as they thus spake, Jesus himself stood in the midst of them, and saith unto them, Peace be unto you."

Luke 24:36

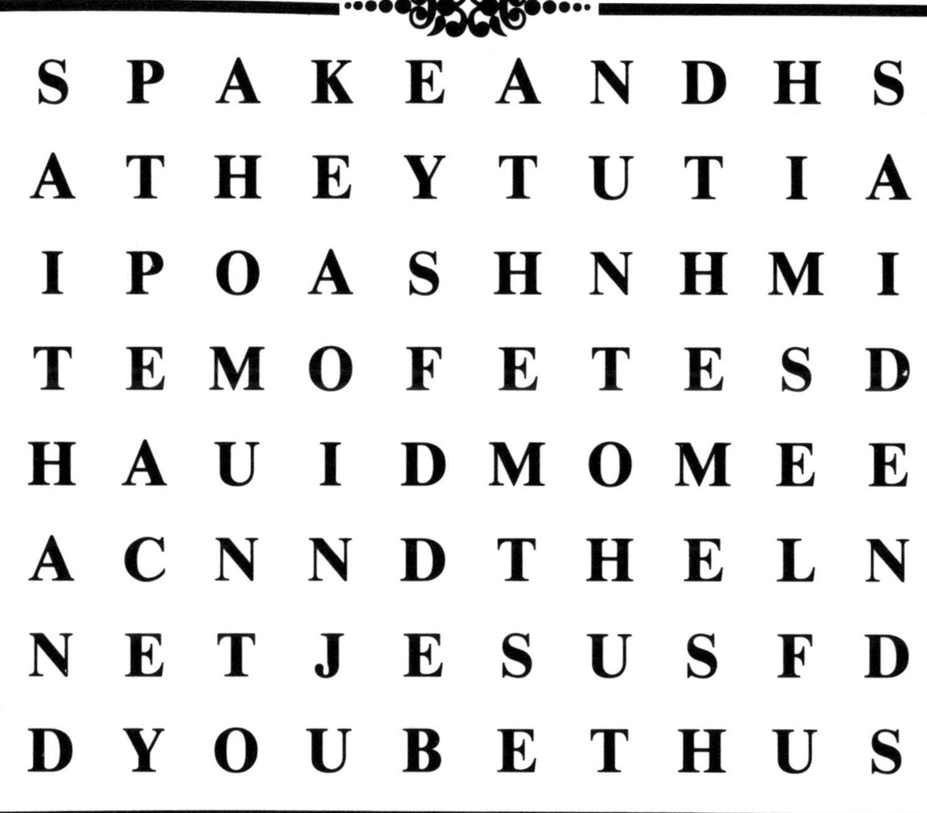

S	P	A	K	E	A	N	D	H	S
A	T	H	E	Y	T	U	T	I	A
I	P	O	A	S	H	N	H	M	I
T	E	M	O	F	E	T	E	S	D
H	A	U	I	D	M	O	M	E	E
A	C	N	N	D	T	H	E	L	N
N	E	T	J	E	S	U	S	F	D
D	Y	O	U	B	E	T	H	U	S

Name________________________________

To discover the secret words, you will need your crayons. Color the spaces with one dot ORANGE. Color the spaces with two dots YELLOW.

Name________________________

DOUBTING THOMAS

John 20:24-29

To discover the secret message, follow the directions carefully.

HTIMDE NDE WIH NOHT HTS

_______ ____ ____ _____ ____

AOECOPLSE NTSW HTSY EDN

_________ _____ ____ ____

JSEUE. TS EDOA, "SXCSPH O

_____ __ _____ ______ _

ETDLL ESS OW TOE TDWAE HTS

_____ ____ ___ ____ ______ ____

PROWH IF HTS WDOLE . . . O

______ __ ____ ______ _

NOLL WIH BSLOSVS."

____ ____ _______

Change all the A's to D's.
Change all the D's to A's.
Change all the E's to S's.
Change all the S's to E's.
Change all the W's to N's.
Change all the N's to W's.
Change all the H's to T's.
Change all the T's to H's.
Change all the I's to O's.
Change all the O's to I's.
The other letters are correct.

Name________________________________

All the vowels in the message below are incorrect. Replace the incorrect vowels with the correct vowels, and you will discover the secret message.

"JASIS SEUTH INTE HEM,

_____ _____ _____ _____

THIMUS, BICEISA THAI HEST

_____ _____ _____ _____

SUUN MA, THIE HUST

_____ _____ _____ _____

BALAUVID: BLASSUD URI THAY

_____ _____ _____ _____

THIT HUVA NIT SAUN, END YAT

_____ _____ _____ _____ _____ _____

HIVA BILEUVAD."

_____ _____

Circle the first letter and then circle every third letter to discover the answer to this puzzle.

ANSWER: _ _ _ _ _ _ _ _ _, _ _ _ _ _ _

_ _ _ _ _ _ _ _ _ _ _ _ _

_ _ _ _ _ _ _ _ _.

T T U H O I O M N M T Y A W E S N B R T
Y E A W A B N C V E H U I H O P I M N T
H E H A S E M N R B V T G H H I M Y M T
F I O I B V N G H G R W E T U R

Name______________________________

THE GOSPEL

John 20:30,31

Use the code found below to solve this puzzle.

N	R	D
G	T	S
M	H	Y

J.	P.	.L
C·	F.	.A
I˙	E.	.U

“______ ______ O______

______ ______ ______

______ ______ ______

______ O__

______ ______....”

Name______________________________

Cross out one letter in each word below to spell the secret message. Then write your own message and put one extra letter in each word. Ask a friend to solve your puzzle.

"BLUT THOESE TARE WRITTENS,

_____ _____ _____ _____

THAET YET MSIGHT BELIEVES

_____ _____ _____ _____

STHAT JESUSS HIS THEM

_____ _____ _____ _____

CHRISTE, THEN SOON OFF GOOD;

_____ _____ _____ _____ _____

HAND THATS BELIEVINGE YET

_____ _____ _____ _____

MIGHTE SHAVE SLIFE THROUGHE

_____ _____ _____ _____

THIS NAMES."

_____ _____

Three letters in this message have been replaced with the letter *X*. Can you decode this message by filling in the correct letters?

XXGXX XOT WRXTTEX XX THXX

_____ _____ _____ _____ _____

BOOK

_____

Name______________________________

SEA OF TIBERIAS

John 21:1-14

To decode this message, use the code found below.

A = B = C = D = E = F =
G = H = I = J = K = L =
M = N = O = P = Q = R =
S = T = U = V = W = X =
Y = Z =

“ , ”

Write a Bible verse in code.

Name____

Finish these magic word squares by spelling words found in the Scriptures. The words must read down as well as across.

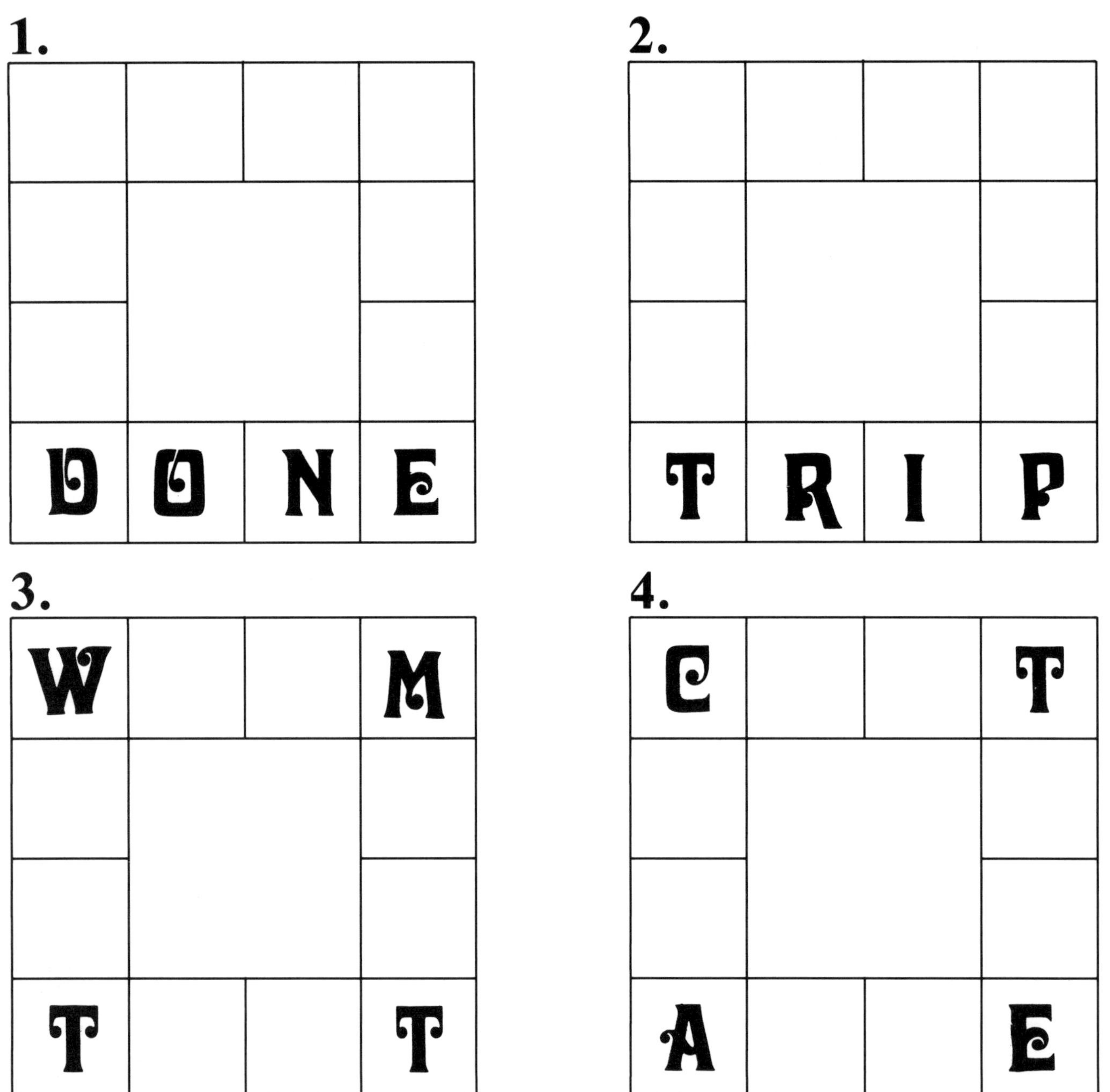

Make up your own magic word squares using words found in the Scriptures.

Name____________________

JESUS TALKS TO PETER

John 21:15-23

To discover the secret message, follow the directions carefully.

SECRET MESSAGE: "_ _ _ _ _ _ _ _ _ _ _ _ _ _ _ _?" "_ _ _ _ _ _ _ _ _ _."

1. A N T L O V E S T P U R P L E

2. G L O R I A Z T H O U F O U R

3. Z C A T M E M A T T H E W Z B

4. Y E L L O W F O L L O W S I X

5. S I M O N Z Z N A O M I M E C

Cross out the girl's name in lines 2 and 5.
Cross out the boy's name in lines 3 and 5.
Cross out the color in lines 1 and 4.
Cross out the animal in lines 1 and 3.
Cross out the number in lines 2 and 4.
Cross out the last letter in lines 3 and 5.
Cross out all the Z's in the puzzle.
Circle all the words that are left.

Name____________________________________

Complete these word stars by spelling words found in the Scriptures. In each star, the words always have the same middle letter.

1.

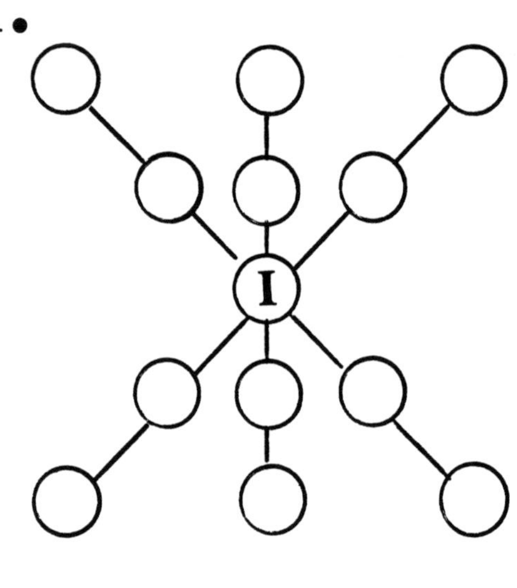

2.

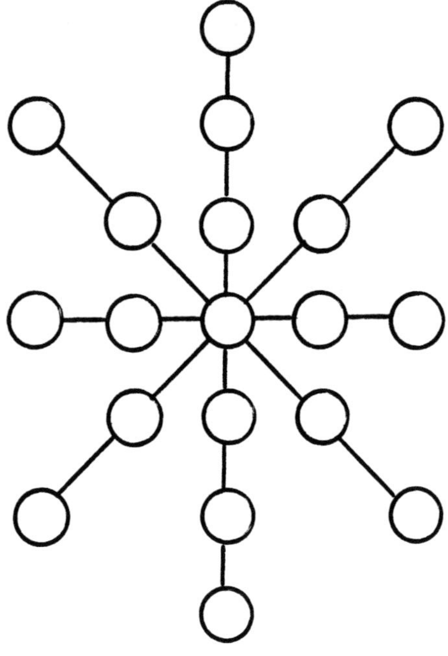

3.

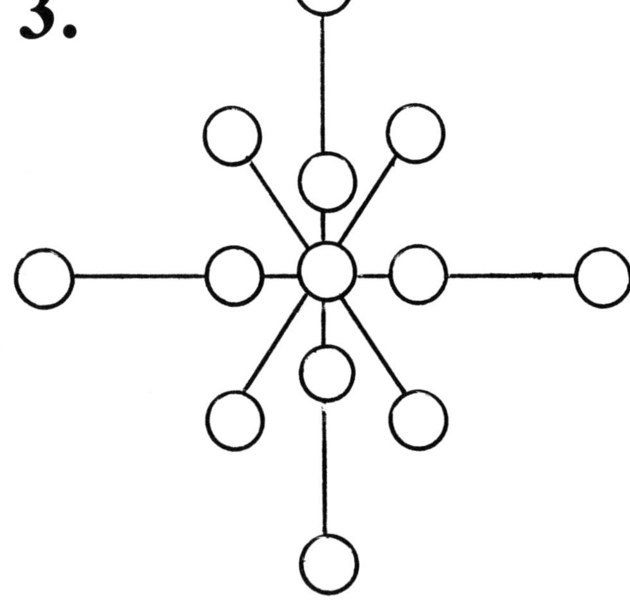

4.

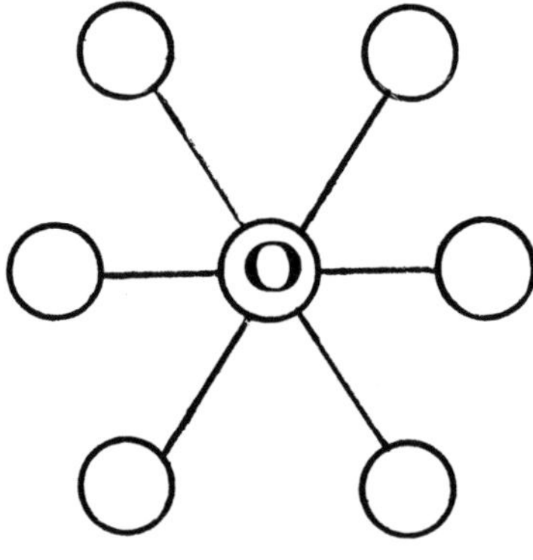

Make up your own word star puzzle using the Scriptures.

Name____

CONCLUSION

John 21:24,25

Each row of jumbled letters found below contains a hidden word. To discover the secret message, circle the hidden words and write them in the order they are found on the blanks below.

SECRET MESSAGE: "This is _ _ _

_ _ _ _ _ _ _ _ _ _ _   _ _ _ _ _ _ _

_ _ _ _ _ _ _ _ _ _ _ _ _ _   _ _

_ _ _ _ _ _ _   _ _ _ _ _ _ _ _ _,   _ _ _ _

_ _ _ _ _ _ _   _ _ _ _ _ _ _

_ _ _ _ _ _ _ _ _...."

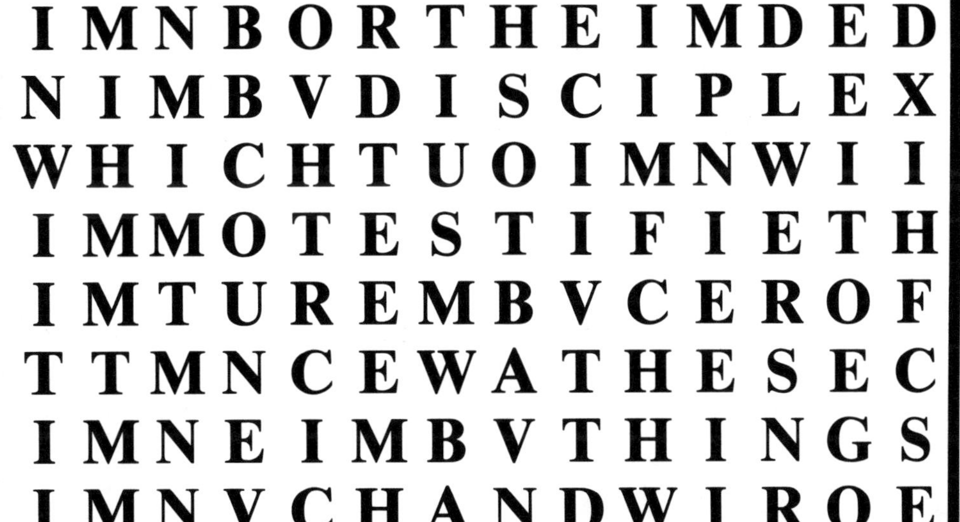

Name________________________________

Can you read this rebus message? Let the Scriptures help you. Then write your own rebus message about this story.

"  al+ 

 +y  Things Which

JESUS did, The WHICH, if

t+  Should  WR + 10

EVERY 1, 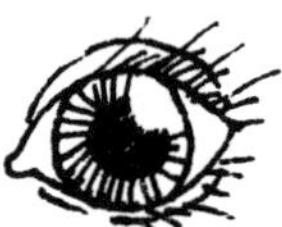 suppose T+ 

even The  ITSELF could

 contain The 

That SHOULD  WR+10. a ."

John 21:25

Name____

INTO HEAVEN

Mark 16:19,20; Luke 24:50-53

To discover the secret message, follow the directions carefully.

SECRET MESSAGE:

"__ __   __ __ __ __   __ __ __ __ __   __ __ __
1 2   3 4 5 6   7 8 9 10 11   12 13 14

__ __ __ __   __ __ __   __ __ __ __ __ __
15 16 17 18   19 20 21   22 23 24 25 26 27

__ __ __ __   __ __ __ __,   __ __   __ __ __
28 29 30 31   32 33 34 35   36 37   38 39 40

__ __ __ __ __ __ __ __   __ __   __ __ __ __
41 42 43 44 45 46 47 48   49 50   51 52 53 54

__ __ __ __ __ __,   __ __ __   __ __ __   __ __
55 56 57 58 59 60   61 62 63   64 65 66   67 68

__ __ __   __ __ __ __ __   __ __ __ __   __ __
69 70 71   72 73 74 75 76   77 78 79 80   81 82

__ __ __."
83 84 85

Put the letter *a* in spaces 7,20,39,57,61,65 and 78.
Put the letter *c* in space 43.
Put the letter *d* in spaces 18,21,48,63,80 and 85.
Put the letter *e* in spaces 5,10,14,26,34,37,42,44,47,56,59 and 71.
Put the letter *f* in spaces 8 and 82.
Put the letter *g* in spaces 74 and 83.
Put the letter *h* in spaces 4,13,19,33,36,55,70,75 and 77.
Put the letter *i* in spaces 45,51 and 73.
Put the letter *k* in space 25.
Put the letter *l* in space 15.
Put the letter *m* in space 35.
Put the letter *n* in spaces 6,27,29,52,60,62,68 and 79.
Put the letter *o* in spaces 2,16,24,31,54,67,81 and 84.
Put the letter *p* in spaces 23 and 50.
Put the letter *r* in spaces 11,17,41 and 72.
Put the letter *s* in spaces 1,22,40 and 64.
Put the letter *t* in spaces 3,9,12,30,32,53,66, 69 and 76.
Put the letter *u* in spaces 28 and 49.
Put the letter *v* in spaces 46 and 58.
Put the letter *w* in space 38.

Name____

Start in any circle and move along circles that are connected by a line. How many words found in Mark 16:19,20 or Luke 24:50-53 can you spell? There are at least 20.

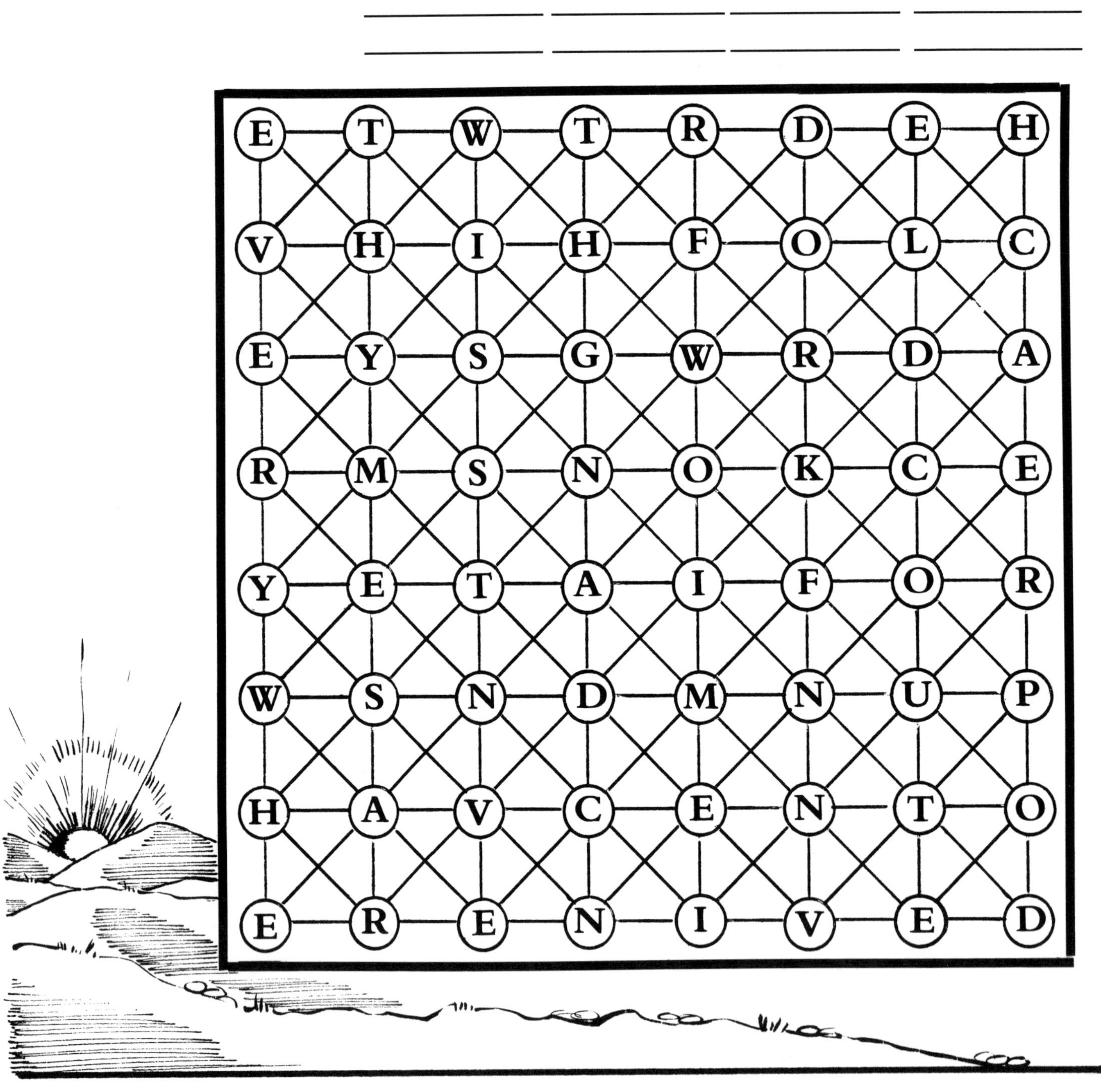

Name____________________________________

REVIEW

John 20:26-31, 21:1-25

Color the spaces YELLOW if they contain statements made by Jesus. Color the spaces GREEN if they contain statements not made by Jesus.

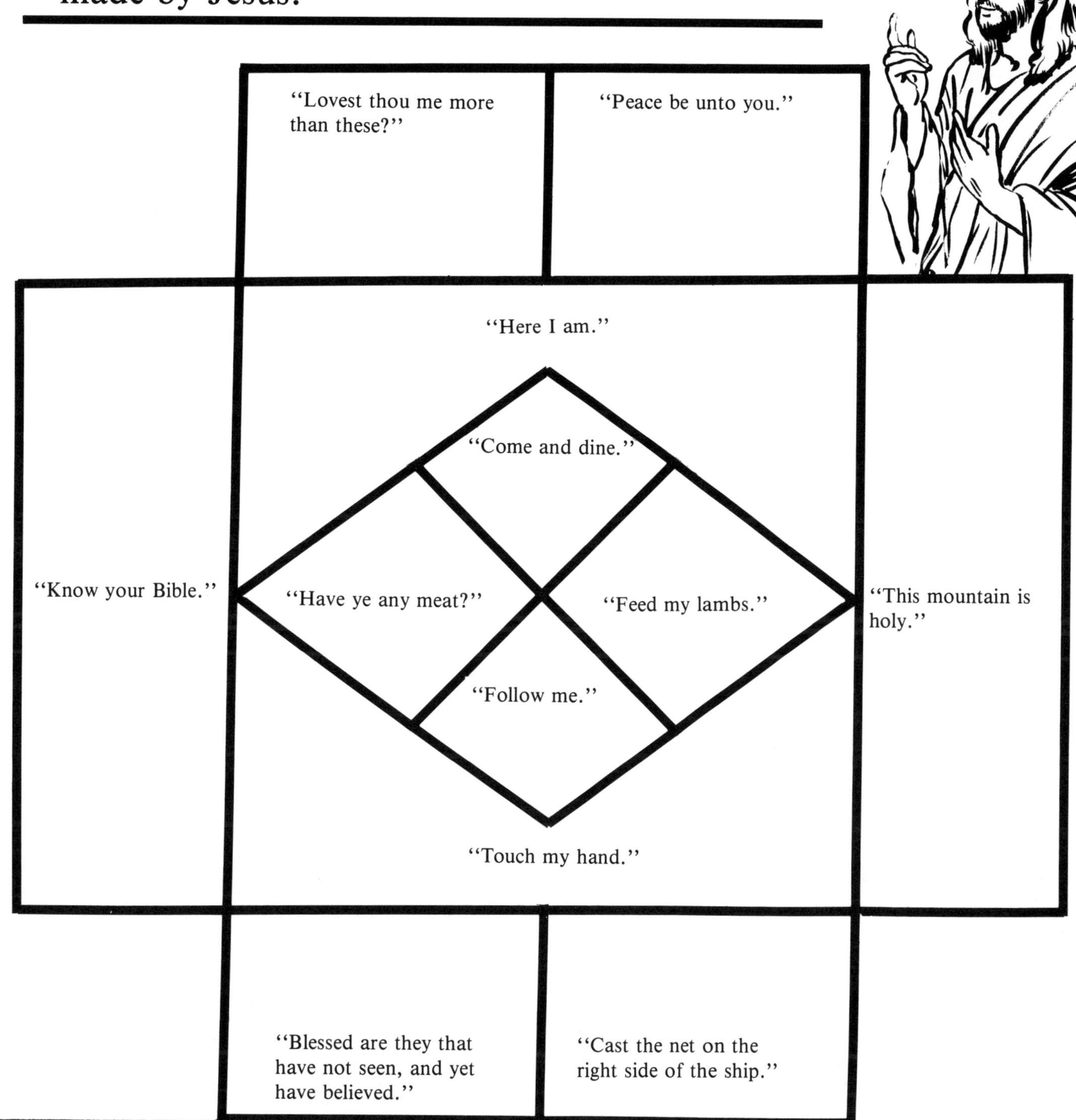

Name____________________________________

PRE AND POST-TEST

Read the statements below. If the statement is true, color the appropriately numbered spaces BLACK. If the statement is false, color the appropriately numbered spaces PINK.

1. After Jesus died on the cross, some of His persecutors realized His divinity.
2. The disciples went to Pilate and begged for the body of Jesus.
3. The chief priests and Pharisees asked Pilate to secure the tomb of Jesus.
4. On the morning of the third day an angel descended and rolled the heavy stone of the tomb away.
5. When Mary Magdalene saw the open tomb, she rushed inside to look for Jesus.
6. On the road to Galilee, some women met Jesus on the road.
7. All the disciples except Peter went into Galilee to wait for Jesus.
8. Thomas did not believe that the disciples had spoken to Jesus.
9. Jesus told the disciples, "I am with you alway."
10. Jesus spoke to Thomas about faith saying, "Blessed are they that have not seen, and yet have believed."
11. Jesus helped the disciples catch a lot of fish in the sea of Tiberias.
12. The disciples did not recognize Jesus at first when He spoke to them from the shore.

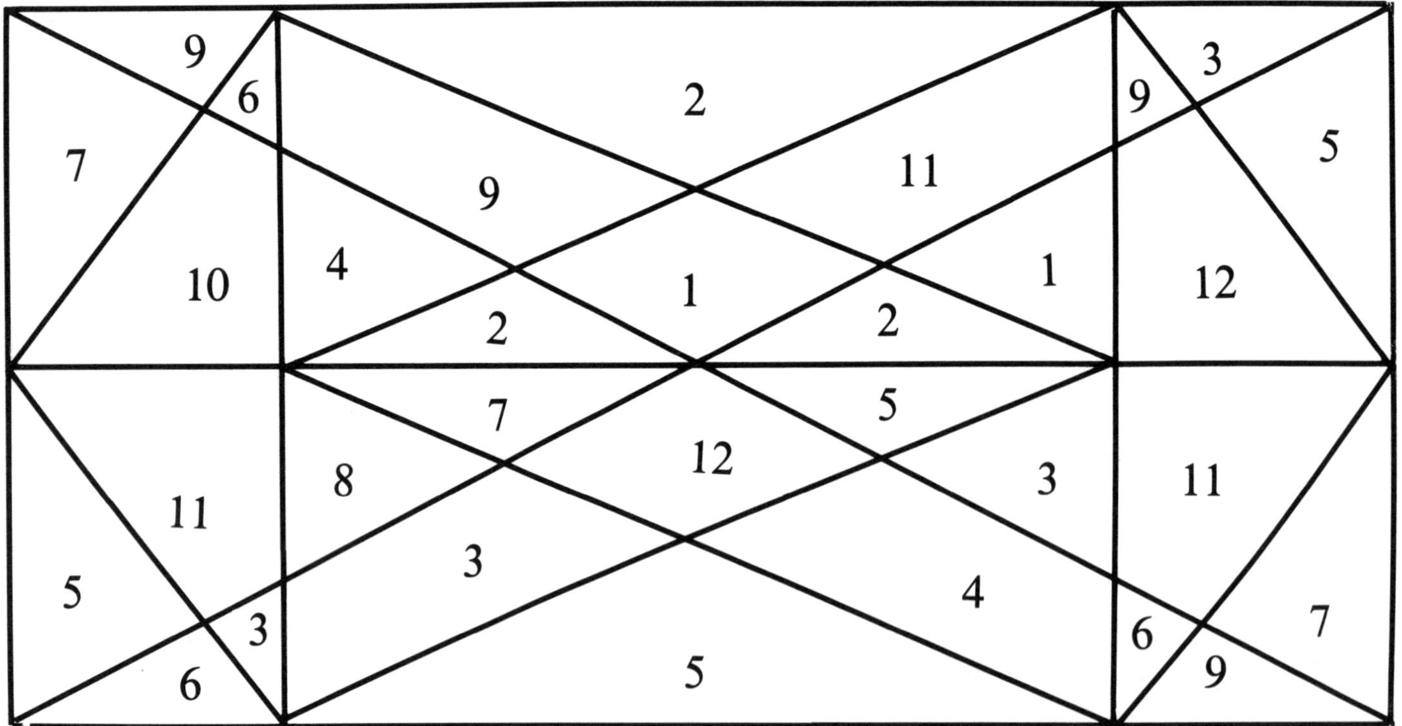

Name____

ANSWER KEY

3. JOSEPH OF ARIMATHAEA

4. MANY WOMEN FOLLOWED JESUS.

M	A	N	Y	W	O	M	E	N	F
A	N	Y	Y	O	M	E	N	F	O
N	Y	W	O	M	E	N	F	O	L
Y	W	O	M	N	F	F	O	L	L
W	O	M	E	F	F	O	L	L	O
O	M	E	N	O	O	L	L	O	W
M	E	N	F	L	L	L	O	W	E
E	N	F	O	L	L	O	W	E	D
N	F	O	L	O	O	W	E	D	J
F	O	L	L	W	W	E	D	J	J
O	L	L	O	E	E	D	J	E	E
L	L	O	W	D	D	J	E	S	U
O	W	E	D	I	E	S	U	U	S

ministering

5. "After three days I will rise again."

6. "Pilate said unto them, Ye have a watch: go your way, make it as sure as ye can. So they went, and made the sepulchre sure, sealing the stone, and setting a watch."

Across:	Down:
2. sepulchre	1. went
4. watch	2. sealing
5. them	3. can
8. said	6. make
9. stone	7. sure

"Make it as sure as ye can."

7. "And, behold, there was a great earthquake: for the angel of the Lord descended from heaven, and came and rolled back the stone from the door, and sat upon it."

8. "He is not here: for he is risen, as he said. Come, see the place where the Lord lay. And go quickly, and tell his disciples that he is risen from the dead. . . ."

They departed quickly.

9. "And as they went to tell his disciples, behold, Jesus met them, saying, All hail. And they came and held him by the feet, and worshipped him."

10. "Be not afraid."
"Go tell my brethren."
"Go into Galilee."
"There shall they see me."
They held him.

11. The elders didn't want people to know that Jesus had fulfilled His prophecy to rise on the third day. So a large amount of money was given to the soldiers as a bribe. The soldiers were told to tell everyone that the disciples had taken Jesus' body from the tomb.

12. B = 7, D = 4, H = 5, M = 6, N = 9, S = 2, T = 3, Y = 8

"And when they saw him, they worshipped him: but some doubted."

some, sum
the, thee
all, awl
by, bye, buy
night, knight
him, hymn
we, wee
to, too, two
you, ewe, yew
counsel, council

13. "I am with you alway."

14. Across:	Down:
1. Father	2. therefore
3. teach	4. Holy
5. you	6. unto
7. Son	9. alway
8. have	10. even
10. end	

15.

S	P	A	K	E	A	N	D	H	S
A	T	H	E	Y	T	U	T	I	A
I	P	O	A	S	H	N	H	M	I
T	E	M	O	F	E	T	E	S	D
H	A	U	I	D	M	O	M	E	E
A	C	N	N	D	T	H	E	L	N
N	E	T	J	E	S	U	S	F	D
D	Y	O	U	B	E	T	H	U	S

16. "PEACE BE UNTO YOU."

17. Thomas was not with the disciples when they saw Jesus. He said, "Except I shall see in his hands the print of the nails . . . I will not believe."

18. "Jesus saith unto him, Thomas, because thou hast seen me, thou hast believed: blessed are they that have not seen, and yet have believed."
Thomas, reach hither thy finger.

19. "And many other signs truly did Jesus in the presence of his disciples. . . ."

20. "But these are written, that ye might believe that Jesus is the Christ, the Son of God; and that believing ye might have life through his name."
signs not written in this book

21. "And he said unto them, Cast the net on the right side of the ship, and ye shall find."

22.

```
d r a w    t h i s
e     i    h     h
a     s    a     i
d o n e    t r i p

w h o m    c a s t
e     e    a     h
n     a    n     e
t h a t    a b l e
```

23. "Lovest thou me?" "Follow me."

24. 1. saith, third, which
2. these, sheep, seeth, stretch
3. again, shall or spake, was, say
4. son, not, God

25. "This is the disciple which testifieth of these things, and wrote these things. . . ."

26. "And there are also many other things which Jesus did, the which, if they should be written every one, I suppose that even the world itself could not contain the books that should be written. Amen."

27. "So then after the Lord had spoken unto them, he was received up into heaven, and sat on the right hand of God."

28. he, was, received, up, into, heaven, and, they, went, forth, preached, everywhere, the, Lord, working, with, them, word, signs, amen

29. Statements made by Jesus:
"Lovest thou me more than these?"
"Feed my lambs."
"Follow me."
"Have ye any meat?"
"Cast the net on the right side of the ship."
"Come and dine."
"Blessed are they that have not seen, and yet have believed."
"Peace be unto you."
Statements not made by Jesus:
"Here I am."
"Touch my hand."
"Know your Bible."
"This mountain is holy."

30. true: 1,3,4,6,8,9,10,11,12
false: 2,5,7

AWARD CERTIFICATE

This is to certify that

____

has successfully completed a study of the resurrection of Christ. The Scriptures covered Matthew 27:54-66, 28:1-20; Mark 15:42-47, 16:1-20; Luke 23:50-56, 24:1-49 and 50-53; John 19:38-42, 20:1-31, 21:1-25.

____

signature (teacher)

____

signature (pastor)

____

date